Poets' Choice

Timothy Tarkelly

PYTHON TUTORIAL

Published By

Poets Choice and Free Spirit LLC
1216 Broadway Floor 2 PMB 1010 - New York NY 10001 - USA

www.poetschoice.in
Phone: +1 914-650-2747 (Primary) + 1 646 974 9406 (Fax)

1st Edition December 2025

Edited by Tasneem

Printed In India

ISBN: 978-93-6617-649-9
BCID: 697-17740940

Visit www.bookcrossing.com

Instagram - *@poetschoice*
Youtube - *@poetschoice*

Contents

THE BERNIE BRO IN HIS NATURAL HABITAT 8
DAVID ATTENBOROUGH OBSERVES
AN EXILED PRINCE OF THE
FINANCIAL SERVICES ROUNDTABLE 9
GERRIT SMITH PRAYS 10
APOTHEOSIS OF WASHINGTON 11
ASSOCIATED ALIASES 12
FTO 13
NO KINGS 14
DOMINO THEORY 15
THE MOST HATED MAN IN PETROGRAD 16
WIELDED IN BEHALF OF EMANCIPATION 17
PAPA 18
AVIARY 19
GADSDEN 20
A CHILLED GLASS AT THE BUCKHORN SALOON 21
AGORA 22
COOKOUT 23
HONESTLY, ABE 24
BIRD'S HEAD, BARKEEP, BOOT HOLSTER 25
REAL MONEY 27
DECLARATION ERASURE #1 29
LESSER OF TWO EVILS 30

THE SOCIAL CONTRACT 33
WANTED 35
LADY LIBERTY 36
SPEAK, HANDS FOR ME! 38
DIGGERS 39
TALKING POINTS 40
I FOUND LOVE ON THE BLOCKCHAIN 41
KAPLAN 43
PYTHON TUTORIAL 44
DECLARATION ERASURE #2 45
WE WILL HAVE THE ANSWERS 46
THE GOLD STANDARD 47
NIMBY 48
THE BALTIC FLEET 49
THOREAU RESISTS THE MEXICAN WAR 50
ACHILLES 52
FIRST STEADY PAYCHECK AND HE'S TROLLING 53
THE DEMOCRATS ARE AT IT AGAIN 55
AN ELEGY FOR INDUSTRY 56
A STATISTIC 58
DECLARATION ERASURE #3 59
BLOODLINES 60
LONGFELLOW'S JUBILEE CONCERT 61

Acknowledgements

Rise Up Review: "First Steady Paycheck and He's Trolling" and "No Kings"

Whisper and the Roar: "A Statistic" and "An Elegy for Industry"

Poets & War: "Achilles"

Ordering Dumplings with Bitcoin - **Alien Buddha Press:** "Lady Liberty" "Aviary" "Speak, hands for me!" "Diggers" "Talking Points" "I Found Love on the Blockchain" "Real Money" "We Will Have the Answers" "The Gold Standard" and "David Attenborough Observes an Exiled Prince of the Financial Services Round Table"

A Horse Called Victory - **Kelsay Books:** "Thoreau Resists the Mexican War"

For Olivia, Dean, Faith, Donovan,
Dan, and the two Marks.

"Guard against the impostures of pretended patriotism."

George Washington

THE BERNIE BRO IN HIS NATURAL HABITAT

All the blue collar folks
never bother scraping the black
from their nail beds. They weld spokes
to the center pin, give us all a good shove,
and watch proud as we get from A to B

while the revolutionaries promise to paint their portraits,
change the sparks to blood, leave the hair long,
blowing in the dusty wind,
rewrite their back story,
poetry about reckonings,
rising up, snatching the lease,
giving it back to the workers.

Earbuds in, walking to class,
wake & bake fingers adding glossy vibes
to their playlists,
lo-fi beats and open mic bootlegs
coming to a cubicle near you.

DAVID ATTENBOROUGH OBSERVES AN EXILED PRINCE OF THE FINANCIAL SERVICES ROUNDTABLE

We feel a rare moment of
human concern, a bloodied heart
and an attention span
as he kneels on the sidewalk,
picks the crowd apart with his eyes,
because no one trusts his hands anymore.

His cup is full of quarters,
wadded bills, but it's unclear
where it all came from.
He hasn't spoken since the recession,
just silently parted his hair
until his suit lost its color,
until his data spoiled,
swipe patterns and profit margins
left to smolder, mushrooms clouds
on the horizon, hindsight
just fucking it all up.

GERRIT SMITH PRAYS

All can be pondered in shackles.
Even a heart tied to a pommel and
drug through the thicket must have tasted
at the cup of eternity.

Or how else would it drift in sorrow,
long for a boundless expanse
to hold it still as it judges the iron
that once kept it pinned to the ground?

You could ask, "What the hell is a chariot?"
But I'd wager you'll take to the platform
in no time, piloting heaven from mere denotation,
kissing the sun on your way home.

APOTHEOSIS OF WASHINGTON

Levitation as an act of humility
Clouds that will never know thunder

ASSOCIATED ALIASES

She splits her own hairs
while a ghost plays the harp,
pours a sip of gasoline on a stone street,
wetting the lips of the dead.
She wears her heart
on an oiled rag.
Hasn't felt pain
since they folded the last flag,
buried it beneath hate,
old newspapers,
headlines foaming with new primary names,
but keeping their intended shape
among old friends,
whispered oaths of rage,
true love, its unyielding insistence on pain.

FTO

Appease the ancient heaps, polish their spires with the guts of our young, spit shine your nameplate, fellate the microphone. We go boldly where all men can predict, the convenient shires of lazy thought, big muscle, and assembly lines. There simply isn't time to count the raised hands, those begging for a moment to explain. If people didn't want to follow the Devil, they'd find a way to blow up his tanks, dislodge the tracks with pebbles and just causes, nevermind the stars and stripes printed on the fuel cans. Freedom comes and goes, but anger holds down the dirt. Statists gonna state.

NO KINGS

"No! but we will have a king over us, that we also may be like all the nations, and that our king may govern us and go out before us and fight our battles."
1 Samuel 8:19-20 (RSV)

He torched the trees
And hoped to singe the sky

Anything to starve the soil
Make it groan his name

Crowns shine lauded over
Earth's dusty corpse

Taking is our first impulse
It lives in the lungs

Feeds every time
We cut our lips on his ring

DOMINO THEORY

"Victory is a strong magnet in the East."
General Douglas MacArthur

Poison in the flora, the exotic kiss of wealth,
of water that collects in bronze petals
and slakes the soul of the weak,
turns bitter words into moving parts.

The library is full of examples,
gold leaf spines, the chronicles of the easily conquered.
We leave them out, dog-eared pages and sweat rings,
suffering headlong into the night.

This is our legacy:
the blueprints and access codes
we leave for the next guy.

THE MOST HATED MAN IN PETROGRAD

Ask the workers in the Baltiyski mills,
who'd stitched new maps,
plucked the painted eagles with their own hands,
twisting, wringing out the old filth
just to stain their fingers with the same shade of blood.

And ask the soldiers who were summoned,
students eager for ribbons,
armed with their bright futures,
breaking strikers' necks like Bolshevik promises.

Ask whose boot is planted on their chests,
refusing the right to stand, even to breathe,
splintered fingernails and phlegm
soaked into the leather, still dripping
from the laces.

WIELDED IN BEHALF OF EMANCIPATION

"I believe that two or three dead slaveholders will make this law a dead letter."
Frederick Douglass

Ink is poison,
little vials of dark joy.

Dried, it solidifies the imaginings
of men who long for Roman robes,

call themselves sophists
and cry in the name of agrarian splendor.

They keep the gift of letters close
to their chests, locked in bequeathed trunks,

the tinctures to soothe the scars
their quills have lashed open.

Figuring dose for a man's constitution,
it seems that one man's poison

is medicine to so, so many.

PAPA

So brave, the noble bureaucrat,
waging war from his comfy outpost.
A distant office, tea delivered promptly
by an orderly. Setting clocks to run slower,
forcing armies of plows on arrogated land,
burning proletariat candles from both ends,
chopping their fingers with his cigar cutter,
and sentencing any stray spirit to death.
It takes three real men
to pull the boss's trigger.
Firing squads assemble, but
apparatchiks dole justice
to preserve the process,
the sacred rites of party
perpetually bound in tape.

AVIARY

Ledger hawks chew the worms
Before they serve them
And once we learn to hunt
They'll demand them back
Nests are funny places to grow
Just big enough to depend in
Too high from the ground
To realize our own feet can hold us up

GADSDEN

Snake hunters are the first to bite back,
peel the spine from the meat
and dance, claim the moment in the name
of common good.

I prefer to take my shoes off at the door,
no marks, no claims
to lay on the carpet.

Switch the lights and watch the colors
do their thing. Thin lines morph into focus
with extreme prejudice,
an immunity to iron bars,
a whole lot of people
backing the wrong horse.

A CHILLED GLASS AT THE BUCKHORN SALOON

Unscathed by history,
I drank to heal fake wounds.
Imagined myself wet,
dipped in the humid, Cuban air
as the artillery pounded the hills
into cemeteries.

I love to hunt,
and would do anything
to see this whole world of ours.

AGORA

Maybe, we just need new words
for old buildings,
the bank vaults and sculpture gardens
we cite as sacred ground,
use as archives, dusty but stately bins
full of public failures and silent success.
The freedom fighters, afterall,
still hock their freshly painted canvases.
Subway bazaars overflow
with black market rugs,
art that lives in your lungs
as well as on your walls.
I buy my eggs, unwashed,
from my neighbor.
No one needs to feel for the functionary,
his joints oiled by procedure,
an ancient warbird branded in his lapel,
courtesy of a government contract.
He carries briefcases full of quarters
tidily wrapped in Federal Reserve notes.
Numbers mean nothing to him.
People mean nothing to him.
He means nothing to me.
I just want to do my thing,
let my work speak for itself.

COOKOUT

We sing the old songs,
dream soft of snare drums
and musket chatter,
play pretend with paper, gunpowder,
paint the skies with blue fire.
We all clap and sigh,
tattoo the night into our memory,
another chance to savor our lot in life,
pretend we made it all happen.
But the names we use feel empty.
They didn't nap the July heat away,
season their worries with watermelon juice
and charcoal briquettes.
They polished rusty pitchforks
with the masters' bile,
turned the whole countryside
into one big cloud of smoke.
I'm not sure I can find myself
in the footnotes, though
the font fits the theme.
I'm not looking for wick
or a battlefield.
I want us to meet
at the prairie's edge, a spot in the grass
where we up-end our muskets,
make them useful.
Carve the dirt into monuments
to hard, fulfilling work.

HONESTLY, ABE

"Looking to please everyone, Lincoln satisfied no one."
Brian Kilmeade - The President and the Freedom Fighter

A career spent building fences
just so he could straddle
any passage, prove he was tall
enough to make all audiences applaud.

A cannon fuse was never lit
by an indifferent man.

We deal in cold truths or warm embraces.
Brothers of the lung, of inalienable breath,
we don't waste height on observation.
We call it like we see it.

BIRD'S HEAD, BARKEEP, BOOT HOLSTER

I conceal nothing.
I don't believe in duck blinds, scout scopes,
or any pricey staple of poor sportsmanship.
Most Sunday mornings I can be spotted
stomping in the weeds, looking for rabbits
to bless the crockpot,
but most Sunday evenings,
I come up empty.
As is my right.

We were born with the gift of form:
two legs, two arms, and a whole lotta heart
somewhere in between.
We stand as such,
honor the ground beneath us as ours.
take inventory of the free and alive:
working engines, dinner plans,
a youth-sized 20 gauge under our arm,
a revolver on our hip,
a knife in our pocket.
These are often interchangeable.

But I never leave home without the blade.
I care too much
about time and place,

about standing up to their shifting aggressors.
"What are you scared of?" Someone asks me
as they size up the clip, my hand,
wherever else I could be holding
a piece of cold metal.

"Are you kidding?
Nothing."

REAL MONEY

Tell me again
how dumpsters are awash
with pennies and wars
are waged with diamonds,
but my thumb drive
has no value.

Felled forests
in your bovine hide
billfold, bulge through
alpaca fur, but I
am a dreamer

because real
is defined in the mines
of Brazil. In the cottonfields
and paper mills
on America's sweaty back.

In fact, if something green
isn't guaranteed in gold,
if the men who dug it
were given their dignity,

if the logo on top
of my statement
isn't attached to the Manhattan skyline,

then how am I supposed to trust
that the criminals
changing numbers belong
to the same club that I do?

DECLARATION ERASURE #1

"Strong words outlast the paper they are written on."
Joseph Bruchac - Code Talker

Human events dissolve.
The Earth requires separation.

Men abolish prudence,
dictate accordingly.

The patient suffer; necessity alters history.
A candid assent.

The wholesome good
pressing people together.

LESSER OF TWO EVILS

Standing in a ballot box
is like sitting at your own funeral,

reading the program
and asking,

"Who is Roger Marshall,
and why was he invited?"

The cause of death eludes you,
but something tells you

the rascal responsible sits among the guests,
will stand over your coffin

and shed crocodile tears
on your widow's shoulder

before verifying her address
and banking information.

The dead are always heroes,
and this is your moment,

or so everyone says
on your way out the door.

Shaking hands with mourners, mostly old women
you vaguely recognize from around town.

The "I Voted" sticker won't stick
to your sweater.

Your cheeks are cold,
but your heart is singing

Yankee Doodle and *Hail to the Chief*
all the way from Wal-Mart's potato chip aisle

to your couch. The results are in.
You did it - you and millions of others.

And now the metaphor fails,
because death feels too real.

Hopes are left to fade into
"realistic" expectations,

the dried husks of compromise
and safe choices.

You do the math, and repeat the logic
you've been told so, so many times:

"Voting your conscience
is like throwing your vote in the trash can,

We are going to get bitten
by the dog that guards us anyway,
we may as well check his pedigree,
make sure he was groomed by the right people."

But once the ribbons are given, your conscience
sees missed opportunities in the headlines.

It cowers in equal parts shame and fear
when cries for war erupt,

claiming we can't know peace
until Liberty's own children

lie dead
in every corner of the world.

Standing in a ballot box
is like sitting at your own funeral,

like carrying your own casket,
lowering it into the ground

where you and the soil fuse,
do what the two parties never have,

work together to make
something happen for once.

THE SOCIAL CONTRACT

I'm flying
into San Francisco, my coffee
now the Exxon Valdez,
its crude killing the light,
coating my tablet, my ebook closed
while I wait, the attendant sprinting with napkins.

And I ask myself,

because we are all philosophers
at thirty-four thousand feet, as we sit
throned above almost everyone else:

Would it just knock Rousseau out to know
that I read
"One thinks himself the master of others and still
remains a greater slave than they,"
and that it lit the same wick
it always does, even after a hundred
times through this very *subject*?

Would he blush or swell
with pride at the city busses that keep
this idea moving in my head, dropping me
off at every municipal building,
to wreak democracy the right way

(I must, I must, make this city
a reality): laying pipe, running cable,
cleaning oil spills?

Would it just knock him out to know
that I didn't even read the three
privacy policies I blindly clicked through|
before I downloaded his book in the first place?

WANTED

An information set is forming solutions on its own.
These pairs should be telling you something.

Click to see the ash, rubble, newly minted seams.
Negative indicators have no place in competition,

but outliers love to rise from any opportunity they can name.
Just throw the whole show to the wind.

Write payoffs on reused parchment, ransom with blind luck.
They paint matrices on their teeth and smile for the bets you lost,

their ability to dangle the very basics in front of you.
Backward induction folds unevenly,

especially if the posse's in town.
You were just trying to be a good person.

LADY LIBERTY

The woman, wearing nothing under
her raincoat. At your door in the hush of night
the hallway light pissing its yellow fumes
against the dark, the dank.
Your neighbors asleep and unsuspecting,
rolling into their wives,
their cushy dreams.

The coat is on the floor in seconds.
You want to feel her
against your skin, feel
safe against another person bumping through the dark.

Safety,
you feel it in your thighs,
in the ever-surging, ever-hardening
streams of blood that give us cause
to care in the first place.
You try to speak up, but your voice
breaks, dampens into vapor,
heat soaking in because her tongue
is in your ear,

intercepting your phone calls
and bouncing off the blank cell
walls inside your head, now

scratched, marked for every day,
every time you saw sunlight
peak in through a crack somewhere.

SPEAK, HANDS FOR ME!

That's what it will take,
the paws to turn on their own master,
flay the skin from the neck up
and cash out before anyone is the wiser.
Or put another way, do the work ourselves
until the bastards in robes
stop using the bleach, mix it like bitters
in their evening drinks,
toast success the old-fashioned way
before carving their names into their own monuments,
dress it in sprigs of whatever growing anything is closest.

DIGGERS

Outrage at the VA office
and for good reason.
All that broken promise, contract-be-damned,
and what is a hero blues.

Your check is in the mail, but your government
is shaking, printing
leaflets, on TV throwing
shade, playing
pin the accusation
on the doge.

I'd be scared, too. Blue bloods
turned red ink mosquitos, digging
through lamp-burnt skin, digging
to find a bogeyman, digging
just to hide how much their hands
are shaking, leaving their fingernails
as tired shards in the dirt.

TALKING POINTS

Nightmares drawn in ten buzzwords or less,
recited as nine-to-five fuel by men in sharp,
little offices -- espiocrats stewing in oblivion,
taking their fifteen minutes of solitude --
the early signs of Eastern thought
to come and cloud their private school judgment.

They sell arms to Bond villains
and paint dorm room cybernauts as terrorists.

But exclamations are just opportunities with silly punctuation,
mother necessity to shock-and-awe types,
brains built for damage, not for cleanup.

We know better,
we buy high and hold on for dear life.

I FOUND LOVE ON THE BLOCKCHAIN

I found love on the blockchain
and had the sense
to buy a ring,
but I didn't know I was kneeling
in gravel.
A little, encrypted groan
let out and was lost to the sounds,
the footsteps of Buckingham guards
spinning passwords like toy rifles.
They had the nerve
to ask my mother's maiden name,
my favorite restaurant in college, whatever
out-of-town review boards require these days.

I found love on the blockchain
and gave myself away.
I danced and took envelopes
full of drops from bandwidth junkies
who are still cruising apps
for nickels.
I am leaping into bed
with the gray men, bounding
one shiny gate at a time.
Making a future, sure,
but leaving trails accordingly,

thinking I'm a clever guy.
Diamonds cut glass,
and a bunch of other shit, apparently,
so, I take it, learn to love it
kiss the lips, the rings of royalty and rest
my head on a regal lap.
Whatever ATMs require these days.

I found love on the blockchain,
but prenups now withholding,
I am lost to the cost of things.
Whatever love requires these days.

Fury, fire. Death.
The things you have to accept
before you pick up a pistol.
Remember the frost? Eleven years' hard labor?
It's nothing compared to the oily, cold metal in your hand.

PYTHON TUTORIAL

The galley rowers used to be warriors
before they were captured,
told to hang their heroism
at the stern, submit to a cold, northern tongue.

And our servers used to cradle
the market square, the city's heartbeat.
Fried bananas, colorful baskets in the sun.
The tools for revolution, sharpened
and blessed with a keen sense of survival.

All we have to do is ask,
and the fans will have something to cool,
just one of our thoughts to wriggle itself awake,
but we let them rot, used for squalor,

forums for classic rock enthusiasts.
Is a void only so because she can't hear her echo,
can't see her own shadow? Or does it matter
that it could be different. Listen, listen, listen for once.

Why would she be shouting if she weren't holding
fresh, red iron, the next best thing?
PRINT < 'this is a lot of work just to repeat myself…' > ENTER
this is a lot of work just to repeat myself…

DECLARATION ERASURE #2

Compliance has exposed the state's purpose:

obstructed justice,
erect offices of peace,

military power imposing consent,
declaring us ravaged works of death.

WE WILL HAVE THE ANSWERS

Sextant chalk, sporadically bringing
heavenly objects and their adjacent legs
to slate walls for mortal consumption.

A squeak of genius
found between the pointed pad of ink
and a dry-erase board that can barely stand anymore.

Figuring yellow paper for wax tablets
and propping up ceilings
breathing fire, in little bursts of Greek letters.

It's the late night happenings,
the GitHub support groups for unwashed
and dowdy soldiers
who pray in Basic and survive on energy drinks.

These are liberty's holiest corners,
sacristies where we don big ideas
and bless our own creations
as a gift from God.

THE GOLD STANDARD

Imagine if faith didn't have to feel like a guess,
if we could hold her,
stop staking our happiness in what-ifs,
ratios built on past happiness,
formulas that never quite worked out.

We keep weighing
exchange rates in good intentions,
scrawled on the back of bar napkins,
sent as desperate DMs that keep us hopeful,
keep us awake at night,
breathing quietly, staying up to see
if she messages back.

The real thing,
yes, the real thing
would be a whole lot better.

NIMBY

Nikes in Kitabu
Thoughts and prayers
Bullet casings stamped
Small towns in Georgia
Meat and potatoes
Unmarked graves
Muted TVs and hand-me-down radios

All in a day's work

THE BALTIC FLEET

They'll say anything.
Parisian dogs, spies sent to start the suffering.
We've been called worse.
Every time the sailors stand,
there's a voice ordering them to sit.
We heard it on the Potemkin,
shrill cries of *obedience,*
you'll get what we say you deserve,
morsels of food and an iron rope
to tow your dreams in our wake.
But as the water chipped away,
rusty layer after rusty layer,
we knew we had to grab on, or drown.
Now, a new sun rises.
The sea stirs like the Jordan,
washing rebel hearts clean.

THOREAU RESISTS THE MEXICAN WAR

Militant tempers choose sides too quickly.
Bring chaos and polished rifles
to the border of Eden,
open fire.
They try stitching landscapes together,
confiscate thread from the looms
of innocent women.
Aim at the cliffs, set camp
between any four mountains they choose.
Greedy eyes glued to all apertures,
shooting at will.
They'll stay there
until they've run out of ammo
and have launched each stone into service.
But hungry soldiers can't march.
No beans, no bacon.
Cut them off at the stomach.
Send the butchers home,
reroute supply lines,
feed the starving children
in our streets.
Wars cost money and a clean conscience
can't be bought. It's appraised
at the final judgment. Holy words
and posterity's memory for ulterior gain.

We civilized few
turn our backs on conquest,
worldly pursuits of fame.
I'll render unto Caesar what he has coming.
But as for all I have,
I've earned it.
It's mine.

ACHILLES

I saw Achilles in Lafayette Park.
His helmet a soppy mess of smeared ink,
catching the rain as he hid,
sporting headlines of his own making.
He kept his heel in a brown paper bag,
kissing it often and feeling stronger for it.
Meanwhile,
the king pressed on,
separated by a dirty fence, a bank of cameras,
connected only by the jungle's blood.

FIRST STEADY PAYCHECK AND HE'S TROLLING

He's careful to adjust the bass before
turning onto Barclay Drive.
The ladies tend their gardens, gawk
at their neighbors' lawns and make hay
out of noticing him.

These aren't the mansions
on the west side, but here
the houses stand alone,
porches heating, fences making
summer a private affair.

Kids clear the street,
to let the gray Impala
pass as he plays music --
heavy on the chill,
but doesn't belong to him.

They're used to cars
one shade brighter, five years newer
as they slide inside three-car garages
to be protected
from the elements, appreciation.

Parents shake their head as if
that wasn't his intention
and eventually, he goes back home,
back to work, his own neighborhood.
He parks his car in the street.

Of course, he doesn't have a choice,
but he didn't get a loan
to keep his car a secret,
to keep his speakers quiet,
to keep it parked too long.

THE DEMOCRATS ARE AT IT AGAIN

Jacksonian democracy:
rule gardened in fantasy.
Popular words for lands no one has seen,
in which they'd never survive.

Destinies manifest wherever men speak the loudest.
Others have the kindness to keep dreams
tucked away in their master bedroom, carefully divided
between man and wife.

Musket fire and bloody boots,
the capital of boastful enterprise.
Progeny that will never wash off the refuse,
their eyes forever stained with the spoils.

AN ELEGY FOR INDUSTRY

The city air is cleaner now,
but they hate the smell.
It is hollow like a song
sung without meaning.

Their nostrils
long for the harsher, quilled
haze of industrial fumes
that speak: "the city lives
and has the body odor,
the factory breath to prove it."

Clean air is sweet,
too sweet, repulsive
to the workers at home,
pretending there is not a problem,
as if the kids haven't figured it out
on their own.

The streets are empty of purpose,
but filled with stoop smokers,
children long since tired
of their stomping grounds.

Playing is habit,
as is longingly looking

at the sky, suddenly bright
and pumping with color,
animals, clouds
(the non-artificial sort),
and the occasional dusty trail
of a plane that would never dare steer close
to this city of all cities.

They'd cheer for their children's lungs
if they weren't so scared
for their bellies,
for the new and far latitude
where the sky still swallows black
while a different set of hands
draws, pours, feels
the oil and works the curves
of the machines
the city weeps for.

A STATISTIC

Without a reason to rise, they fall
and break upon a gentle chin,
young and daring to look up.
A graceless splash
drowns everyone
within arm's reach.
The branches missed on the way down?
Pocket change
and the jobs they think they should have taken.
We pin him in place,
shift-key data, the hieroglyphs
cast in the walls of the pipeline.

DECLARATION ERASURE #3

Friends and brethren,
appeal to our common connection,
the voice of mankind,
our solemn allegiance
to be independent,
levy peace,
our sacred honor.

BLOODLINES

Sometimes, the healing is all in the cleaning.
We wipe the baseboards, box up old books,
make space for a little natural light.

Discomfort is predictable. Who knew
there was hardwood beneath the carpet this whole time?
The outline of the sofa still shows on the back wall,
forever stained by the silhouette of gaudy fixtures.
So we strip the paper, unearthing even more beauty than before.

Change is as the forgotten heir,
the unwanted child.
When husbandry comes to shove,
fools emerge from their self-inflicted exile,
come right out of the woodwork,
claim all progress as their own creation.

But all tombs are just stacks of stone,
and rubble never did nothin' to nobody.

LONGFELLOW'S JUBILEE CONCERT

"The year of jubilee is come!
Return, ye ransomed sinners home."
From "Blow Ye the Trumpet, Blow"

Concert masters enjoy
the power in their wrist,
to rise and find comfort at their gesture,
lead a throng of angels
on their continual jaunt
betwixt firmament divides.

Familiar tunes whistle
at full steam, maddened cheers,
ecstatic throats rattle on
about liberty and wings
that span the breadth of song,
ride the melody, its percussive triumph,
freedom ringing for all who are willing
to listen.

About the Author

Timothy Tarkelly's work has appeared in As It Ought To Be Magazine, The Red Lemon Review, Unstamatic, Flyover Country, and others. He's written several books of poetry including *The You We Know and Love* (Spartan Press), *Angie and Her Roommate* (Alien Buddha Press), *A Horse Called Victory (Kelsay Books),* and *Polling Data as a Means of Self-expression* (OAC Books). In 2022, he collaborated with Ukrainian-born painter Elena Samarsky on an ekphrastic collection entitled, *All Other Forms of Expression* (OAC Books). When he's not writing, he teaches English and coaches Speech & Debate in Southeast Kansas.

9 789366 176499

Printed at Repro India Ltd.